BODY TALK:
The Body Language Skills to Decode the Opposite Sex, Detect Lies, and Read Anyone Like a Book

By Patrick King

Social Interaction Specialist and Conversation Coach at www.PatrickKingConsulting.com

Table of Contents

4

Introduction

I started volunteering with children on the **autism spectrum** when I was a teenager and continued to do so through my college years.

It was an activity that admittedly started with an eye towards bolstering my college applications, but soon uncovered a genuine passion I had for helping people. And I suppose this somewhat foreshadowed my current career and professional interests...

It was incredibly gratifying to work with children one-on-one and help them develop the simple skills that other children could pick up instinctually. Seeing weekly progress and growth was something of a driving force for my college work with autistic kids, and was very nearly a career choice. The thankfulness and pure gratitude of the parents was also something that I'm not likely to forget in my life.

But working with a population like that was not without its hardships and was often thankless – this is where body talk and body language comes into play.

Aside from weekly nail scratch marks and occasional bite marks, a hallmark of those on the autism spectrum is the **inability to read social cues**, of which body language is an integral part.

I discovered this for myself on my first day, when I found that my attempts at sarcasm and humor were met with blank stares or very literal interpretations.

Any further attempts of conveying a message through any means other than a literal interpretation of the words failed, and it dawned on me how much of communication was natural, non-verbal, and based on body language and mutual assumptions.

It's like using a series of sports analogies to

explain something to someone, but they aren't familiar with any of them.

So while this realization definitely taught me to be more precise and exact with my words, the prevailing lesson I walked away with was just how much of communication is conveyed non-verbally and through our body language.

Professor Mehrabian of the University of Pennsylvania conducted a landmark study that found that physical (body language) signals comprise a majority of the communication that we send to others, coming in at a whopping **55%**.

How much did the actual words coming out of our mouths account for? A mere **7%**, with vocal tone and inflection checking in at **38%**.

This is a startling realization, but not one that should alarm you. Professor Mehrabian made two additional discoveries about body language.

First, that much of body language was universal throughout the world and its varying cultures... and even the animal kingdom as displayed in apes and monkeys.

<u>Second</u>, that much of body language was also innate, as shown in blind people exhibiting many of the same gestures and body language signals that sighted people do.

So even if 55% of our communications are unconscious physical gestures and body language signals, most of us have a decent **baseline** in our non-verbal communication skills because many are simply innate to human nature.

But a *baseline is just a baseline*, and simply remaining at a baseline level of skill isn't the focus of this book or the reason you're reading it.

Unlike rules of conduct and courtesy, we're never really taught much about the world of body language and just how to navigate it successfully to do two things: **(1)** read between the lines of what people are actually saying, and **(2)** send out accurate messages with our own body language.

That's exactly what I strive to do in this book.

It makes no attempt to be exhaustive, and focuses on a few of the major body language signals that are used on a daily basis for maximum usefulness. And of course, *attraction and lie detection 101* are always on the mind when we think about body language.

I'll take you through the basics of the physiology of different types of body language, the importance of context, and how intent doesn't always match up externally.

Most importantly, I'll explain how body language signals are just like words in a sentence, and can have entirely different meanings in different sentences. They are often paired with supporting or conflicting signals which must be read together as an entire body language **cluster**.

It's a process. It takes practice. But if you've ever been told *"Oh... I had no idea that's what you meant..."* by anyone, then you know exactly how easily things can be misconstrued.

It's time to learn to listen to other people's body talk, and make sure your body talks exactly what you want it to!

1. Why listen to body talk?

Are you sitting in public right now?

If you are, lock onto someone across the room and try to *read* them. Without being able to hear them or read their lips, can you tell what emotion they are feeling? Are they frustrated and annoyed, or radiating joy?

It's easier to guesstimate what they are feeling than you might think!

It turns out that most of the communication we convey to others is non-verbally through our body language, and not that much actually depends on the words that come out of our mouths.

It is how other people can tell what you *were* feeling, *are* feeling, and *will* feel in the future... and how there's a good chance that you can tell what that random stranger across the room is feeling.

Without even knowing it, you use so much more than just your words to get your message across, which sometimes results in your sending a message far different from your intended one. These secondary signals can often be 100% unconscious and escape your awareness completely.

This is obviously a losing proposition, given the gravity of some of the conversations that life throws our way.

The tone of your voice, facial expressions, how you move your hands, and certain body language signals can send people a message that may or may not support the words coming out of your mouth.

What if you did this in an important interview, or when you were proposing to the love of your life?

"Melissa, will you marry me?"

"Oh... you were serious? You used such a sarcastic tone of voice..."

Body language is a comprehensive collection of unspoken signals that you send out with your body non-verbally. Maybe it's just your habit or particular way of nodding your head.

People may not realize the signals, but they will read them regardless... and if you don't learn how to send congruent signals, people can and will pass judgment on you.

And there's a good chance that judgment will be incorrect!

It's a good idea to understand why body language is important so you can take steps to actively monitor and control your body language. At the very least, you should be aware of the body language signals you are sending out so you can prevent yourself from sending out the wrong signals.

This chapter is a long and complex way of saying that effective communicators know all of these subtle body language signals, and can control their own with expert discipline. In fact, they go out of their way to ensure that all of their secondary body language signals are exactly consistent with the spirit, meaning, and purpose of the words coming out of their mouths.

They will never send out mixed messages, and what you see and hear is what you get with them.

If you want to be able to communicate more effectively to benefit your relationships and career, you need to master body language!

Four reasons why body language is important.

First, people factor body language into their overall impression of you.

Human communication is a holistic exercise, and isn't just the words coming out of your mouth. Communication is also how you move your hands, the look in your eyes, and your facial expressions. People assemble all these different signals together into an overall impression of the message that you are sending out... and an overall impression of **you**. You are the sum of all of the communication signals you send out.

It's commonly accepted that we assemble everything we notice about a person into a complete assessment of them.

But if you tried to describe all of the reasons that you came to that assessment, it would be tough to articulate. You might talk about how their voice was a little rude, or how their arms made them appear standoffish... but what else?

Therein lies the power of body language and non-verbals – most of the time, they are picked up subconsciously. And that's what makes body language so powerful and frustrating at the same time. People normally lack awareness and don't admit that they've factored body language into their decision about others... but it's often more powerful than the words people speak.

Ever hear someone say *"I just didn't like their vibe"* when describing someone that they've met for all of 30 seconds?

That's it.

It might be latent, but people are heavily influenced by the signals that others send out with non-verbally, so you must be careful and be aware of how you act when you are trying to communicate.

Second, lacking body language awareness can set you back.

In most situations, especially with new people, others are just trying to understand your character. Once they understand your character, they will usually make a quick judgment about whether they like you and want to invest more time in getting to know you. It's a sad but realistic truth.

When people judge you, it is based primarily on **(1)** what others say about you, **(2)** what you yourself say, and **(3)** your body language and non-verbals.

Guess which of those 2 you can control?

At the most basic level, you can either give

create comfort or discomfort with your body language signals. If you can make that great, comfortable impression verbally and non-verbally, people will seek to enforce those positive impressions they have of you.

People are more efficient and quick to judge than they realize – much of it of course, being subconscious. We are always on the lookout for those that we like and dislike, and body language can either propel you ahead or set you back with people.

Third, great body language will propel you forward.

In contrast to the previous point, great body language can rescue you even if you say the wrong thing at the absolute wrong time.

You can project strength, humor, humility, sarcasm, charisma, and a host of positive adjectives that we all aspire to. And again, this can be *in spite* of what you actually say. It takes the pressure off always having to be witty and say something clever.

If you consistently control your body language,

you can project a message consistent with your verbal message. This makes you appear more authentic, sincere, and honest. In a business context, this strengthens your bargaining position and makes you a tougher adversary to negotiate with. In a relationship context, you will be able to avoid many games simply by being straightforward and not sending mixed messages.

Finally, your body language affects people's perception of you.

As I mentioned prior, people are always making snap judgments subconsciously. People are trying to figure out where in relation you are to them in the social hierarchy, so they know whether they want to invest more time in you.

They look at your clothes, shoes, how you talk, your accent, your facial expressions, your body language, and your word choices.

Then all of these factors go into a black box, which spits out a sheet grading your class, character, and general value and worth.

The value of how your body talks – your body language – is simply incalculable. We've all heard that you will get ahead in life according to who you know... but that's only half the battle. You really get ahead in life according to who you know, and who likes you.

Learning great body language for yourself, and learning to decode others, will get you most of the way to people simply liking you. Otherwise, regardless of your actual accomplishments and regardless of how good of a person you really are, you may convey that your accomplishments are worthless, and you're not that great of a person after all.

Of course, remember that this is a book of possibilities, and not a book for exact meanings. Everyone is different as a result of their experiences and perspective, so an act for someone may be different for someone else.

2. Everyday body language quirks.

I'll probably repeat this 10 more times before the end of this book, but so much of body language, both our processing and expression of it, is subconscious.

It is subconscious because most of it has been naturally ingrained in us for years... so we think nothing of it.

Sometimes these body language signals are just an automatic response when we have nothing else to say, and there's nothing wrong with that.

However, it's extremely worthwhile to examine what some of these everyday body language signals can mean to others, and how we can bulletproof them to ensure that you are sending the correct message. You don't want to put yourself in a position where you're saying one thing, but your body language signals are saying the opposite.

You'd be surprised as to how many people fail to get that dream job because they are unaware of the body language signals that they are sending out.

You might be **less** surprised at how many people miss out on developing a relationship with someone special because of misinterpreted body language signals – after all, flirting is all one intentionally yellow light.

Paying attention to these common body language quirks will make you a better communicator, hands down. It's more than a matter of aligning your verbal and non-verbal messages – it's delving into how these signals can be misinterpreted by others and completely undermine your character or people's perception of you.

The shrug.

Shrugging has many meanings and is almost

24

always context-dependent.

If you are in unfamiliar territory or a somewhat threatening social situation, a shrug indicates defensiveness and discomfort. This is especially so if the shrug is held, which is a position that indicates stress. Many people carry their stress and anxiety in their shoulders unconsciously, and often have tense shoulders if they are under stress at work.

In other contexts like when faced with someone aggressive or confrontational, it can indicate submission.

It can be as simple as someone attempting to communicate that they don't want to dominate a situation, so they acquiesce and simply show acceptance as subtly as possible.

It can also be your amazingly passive-aggressive friend indicating that they are okay with a choice externally... but barely holding inside their annoyance and contempt.

Shrugging can be an honest "I don't know," or "I don't care," or a subtle opposite effect when paired with a wide-eyed sigh.

Shrugging is an everyday body language quirk that you must be sure to pair with appropriate secondary body language signals, otherwise it can convey a gamut of negative emotions.

The furrowed brow.

A furrowed brow is when people lower their eyebrows down and to the center in an expression that appears annoyed or angry.

If someone has their head lowered, is looking slightly down, and has their brows furrowed, it is normally an indication of a negative mood.

It can even indicate a certain level of aggression or negativity towards a situation or person.

If you pair a furrowed brow with a frown, it can drastically change the perception and is almost always a sign of displeasure and potential anger.

The raised head.

When the person you're talking to raises their

26

head, sticks their chin out, and they seem to be looking at you down from their nose, a lot of different signals are being sent out.

You have to look at the context to get into the reality behind this gesture.

It's a dominant pose where they are literally trying to look down on you, and often when people assume dominant posture, it's a result of insecurity. They try to look fearless when deep down they feel inadequate and not up to the job.

Of course, if you have more context about how that person is feeling, a raised head might actually be a sign of triumph and pride. Finally, it can indicate actual confidence and security.

Or maybe their neck is just stiff from sleeping on a lumpy pillow their night before.

The tight-lipped smile.

When somebody is smiling but their lips are pressed together tightly and they're not showing teeth, this means that they are concealing something. Their eyes might not move, and this tight-lipped smile might be paired with a furrowed brow.

In most situations, this means that they're holding back their real opinion. This gesture is really a polite way of smiling when you don't really want to.

The person may not actually approve of you, or doesn't really look at you that positively, but they just want to be polite. When people have a tight-lipped smile, this is normally a form of emotional lying. They're basically just forced to smile.

The smirk.

A smirk is when one side of the face is smiling and the other side is either frowning, sad or neutral. Usually when people smirk, it's because they find something curious in a negative way, or they're expressing sarcasm.

In certain situations, it also means they're conflicted. They don't really know how to feel about a particular person or a particular conversation, or topic.

It can show a combination of amusement and skepticism as well.

Finally, if you pair a smirk with wide open eyes, it demonstrates annoyance or annoyed shock. Paired with a raised eyebrow and a smirk indicates curiosity or skepticism. Paired with a frown and a smirk is a very clear sign of displeasure and annoyance.

The real smile.

A real smile shows your upper teeth, and your eyes will usually squint and shrink. There will also be wrinkles, otherwise known as smile lines, on the sides of your eyes.

It shows you have nothing to hide and that you're at least attempting to smile sincerely. And of course, it shows entertainment and joy.

This is a rare clear body language signal where there are few interpretations... except the following: in some cases, a real smile might preface a negative feeling, such as laughter out of despair.

Fake smiles on the other hand are all too easy to spot when you know what to look for. A fake smile shows both upper and lower teeth, and the eyes remain unchanged and wide open.

A fake smile will also fade immediately from a person's face and the face will revert back to a neutral expression, whereas a real smile will fade over a series of seconds.

The supported head.

Imagine you're at a table and you rest your head or chin on your hand. This can be interpreted in a host of ways.

First, it can signal boredom, and that you can barely stay awake without keeping your head supported like by something.

Second, it can signal that you are enthralled by a conversation because you are supporting your head to settle in for the long haul. You want to be able to listen for hours.

Third, it can signal that someone is tired of the conversation, but not necessarily because of you. They might have just had a bad night's sleep or long day at work.

Finally, they might have picked up the habit of putting their head on their hand to literally keep their mouth shut and from saying something they might regret – signaling annoyance and anger.

This is by no means an exhaustive list of everyday body language quirks, nor the meanings they can have.

But that wasn't the objective of this chapter.

The objective was simply to introduce a few, examine some of the ways that they can be interpreted according to context, and make sure that you possess the awareness. With your own body language expression, awareness is really half the battle in ensuring that you present yourself how you imagine you do.

If suddenly, in your country, a thumbs up became equivalent to a middle finger, how much better would you fare if you had that simple awareness?

There are very few universal and objective standards for body language. But there does exist a venn diagram of universal signals and meanings that I am seeking to present to you in this book.

3. Body talking trust and empathy.

You might not keep up with current events or even know who your state's governor is (luckily, I had the greatest governor of all time recently – the Governator), but you've surely caught a glimpse of politicians trying to work a crowd and shake hands.

Politicians all tend shake your hand, make certain facial expressions, and use similar gestures. This is no accident, and they are 100% aware of what they are doing.

There are certain body language signals that impart the feelings of trust, authority, and empathy – all things that politicians wish they could bottle up like a fine French cologne.

Knowing these body language signals can go a

long way in helping you get promoted more, get better jobs, or meet more members of the opposite sex. If you want to succeed socially, it's always a good idea to learn certain body language gestures that will help you create a positive first impression, and make people around you more receptive to you.

Body talkin' trust.

It should be noted that these gestures will differ in cultures and location... but I'll cover that in a later chapter.

Let's stay in the land of the west for now, since imperialism is a tough nugget to stop.

A firm handshake is absolutely necessary.

Note the use of the word "firm," and not "strong." A "strong" handshake actually sends a very different signal than a firm handshake. A strong handshake, one that almost breaks bones or makes hands numb, is usually interpreted as some sort of play for dominance by someone who is insecure and/or weak themselves.

Even if you disagree, these are the assumptions that people will make based solely from body language.

A firm handshake is reminiscent of the Goldilocks "*just right*" corollary. Not too weak, not too strong, but just right. Somewhere in the middle.

A firm handshake paired with raised eyebrows and strong eye contact is the key. Raised eyebrows show vulnerability and communicates that you are friendly and intend no harm. It also communicates trust, and so does eye contact in this context.

Trust can be also inferred from open hand gestures with your palms pointing up and wrists exposed. Evolutionarily, having your palms up with your wrists exposed was an amazingly vulnerable position to be in. You could have your wrists slit in a second by a vicious predator, and it is difficult to defend yourself with your palms up.

Inherently, people still recognize this, so when you do this, it signals vulnerability, openness, and trust. You have nothing to hide and you come in peace.

Real smiles induce trust.

Try to control your arm crossing and avoid leaning back from a conversation partner.

Finally, wrap your hands around their hand when you give them a handshake.

You see this in politicians constantly. When you reach out with your open palm to shake their hand, they wrap your hand with both hands. This signals intimacy, acceptance, and support. Even with politicians and salespeople, this helps create familiarity, even though you know deep down that they are trying to gain something from you. You can't help but fall prey to the emotional effects, and that's body language at its best.

Body language signals used to establish trust and empathy are not one-shot bullets. You can't just take one gesture, execute it, and expect to project the right kind of impression. It has to be in context, all the signals have to be aligned, and other body language signals have to be paired properly.

4. Legs set your body talk stage.

Body language is usually born out of simple habit.

Being that we can't always see our legs, body language of the legs is especially habitual and subconscious.

For example, it's why people tend to fidget with their legs so much and jiggle them. It might not indicate anxiety, but it definitely means some emotion is being felt inside and only being expressed externally.

So while I am going to touch upon some common leg body language signals, there are a host of additional ways to interpret them.

Legs frame you.

While facial expressions, eye positioning, and eye activity mean a lot, your overall presence is directly impacted by what you do with your legs.

It is your foundation and builds your posture, and you have to remember that your posture communicates how much power you feel that you have.

It communicates how confident you are and whether you *lack* confidence. The way you stand and the straightness of your posture speaks a lot regarding your respectability, your place in terms of dominance and your comparative strength compared to the people around you.

Weaker framing, stances, and poses will be used in the presence of those perceived to be stronger and more influential than yourself.

A strong stance with minimal fidgeting, shoulder-width apart, and knees locked will convey confidence and power.

Toe positioning.

Your toe positioning indicates your priorities.

If your toes are positioned in such a way that they are pointed at the speaker or the person that you are interested in, this shows that you are paying attention to that person. This shows that you are taking that person seriously or you respect that person. However, if your toes are positioned at an exit or you are shaking your toes, this means that you are either evasive, or you just don't want to be there.

This is extremely important to understand in the context of a date or a job interview. If you want to be taken seriously, you might want to redirect your toes away from the exit and focus it on the person interviewing you. The toes also signal how interested someone is in you, romantically or professionally.

Crossing legs.

When you are standing, there are many ways to position your legs. You can position your legs parallel to each other and never cross them, or you can cross your legs while standing up, putting most of the weight on the back leg.

If you cross your legs, it has been shown to indicate submissiveness and a lack of strong will. You may look to some people that you can be easily swayed, and that you don't have strong convictions... at least regarding whatever the topic of conversation is.

Of course, if you add shifting your weight from foot to foot, it just looks like you need to urinate – which is also easily confused with anxiety and nervousness.

Regardless, crossing the legs can indicate insecurity, defensiveness, passiveness, and overall weakness.

If you're getting a feeling that this section is more confusing than elucidating, welcome to reality. Body language is subjective, but there are high probabilities of what specific signals mean according to the context.

If someone crosses their legs, it's likely that a feeling of discomfort, at the very least, is present and you should change your message and act accordingly.

Wide foot stance.

A wide foot stance refers to when people are standing with their feet apart, knees straight, toes pointed forward, and legs parallel.

It's essentially a neutral position, which means that you have to look elsewhere for indications of how to read them. A wide foot stance is a blank slate, which means one of two things.

First, that they don't feel strongly one way or another, or **second**, that they have managed to control their leg body language, and their true feelings will manifest elsewhere.

The most common place for it to really show up is through the hands. I'll get into this a bit more in the next chapter, but here's a brief summary of hand positioning.

Hands can be hanging at their sides, clasped front of them, clasped behind them, crossed, or gesturing. Each of these can mean very distinct feelings.

For example, if hands are hanging at their sides, studies have shown that it indicates defensiveness. There might have been something that was to their dissatisfaction, and they wanted to say something but didn't. Pair this with the hands being stiff, and you likely have an angry person. Pair it with clenched fists, and you have an enraged person!

If hands are clasped behind them, it can show confidence. They could be supremely comfortable around you and not threatened by you – hence leaving themselves defenseless and at your mercy. It can also show thoughtfulness and that someone is pensive.

If hands are crossed, it is likely that other body language matches that of someone that is either shrinking away, or just doesn't want to be in the situation. It indicates a lack of confidence, boredom, or anxiety.

On the other hand, if there is great posture paired with crossed arms, that person is probably confident and feels a degree of control over the situation. They aren't trying to dominate, at least not outwardly.

How you stand, how you point your toes, as well as what you do with your hands speaks volumes regarding your state of mind. This might not reflect your real state of mind, but it is definitely in your best interest to make sure that your body language signals aligns completely with the specific message or impression you are trying to create in the minds of others around you.

5. Arms, hands, and openness.

As we've learned by this point, communication is not entirely conscious. The key to presenting a cohesive message to others is paying attention and learning about how the feelings of other people manifest in their bodies... and yours.

Important and often subconscious body language signals come through the arms and hands.

They primarily concern the emotions of openness and the tendency to be receptive to new ideas, people, and situations. If you're in a new social situation and you're not sure what to make of it, just look down at what your hands are doing and they will instantly signal how comfortable you are. You can see this manifested in other people as well.

They signal comfort or the lack thereof. Being closed or open with your arms and hands is quite literally the difference between defending yourself from an enemy, or welcoming them with open arms.

Remember, when people detect inconsistencies with your body language or words, it's a slightly unsettling feeling that they won't even realize until they try to explain how they feel about you, and they just say there's something off about you. You don't want people to get the wrong impression of your character simply through habitual gestures that may not fully reflect who you really are.

Regardless of your motivations, here are the baseline hand and arm gestures and signals that you need to be aware of.

There are a lot of relatively obvious hand signals because we use our hands to express our feelings through gestures. Again, this list is not meant to be exhaustive, and should serve primarily to bring awareness to the variety of associated emotions with some body language signals, and become accustomed to the fact that they can be completely different and subjective with different people!

<u>Rubbing your hands together.</u>

You're probably excited about something and expecting that you will come into good fortune. It's a sign of anticipation, and can shine the spotlight on what a person truly wants to happen.

People generally respond favorably to people who rub their hands together if the outcome of that gesture benefits everybody or is part of a contest. However, if you tend to rub your hands and you are talking about business deals, this can lead to misunderstandings.

If you were to rub your hands very slowly and you are talking about a business plan, it may seem that you are trying to be clever. It may seem that you are trying to be underhanded or otherwise sneaky. This is usually not a good sign. People might think you are unethical.

Hand clenches.

A hand clench is when you clench each hand individually, or press your hands together with some pressure.

Hand clenches can mean many different things. It can indicate boredom. But depending on the context, it can also indicate that there is a level of anxiety or frustration in your mind. At worst, it's a signal of anger, and wanting to keep the anger at bay physically so you don't say the wrong thing.

Many times, anxiety and anger have a way of manifesting physically without us knowing – it's a common phenomenon when people suddenly start bleeding from their palms only to realize that they had been clenching their hands so tightly that their nails dug into themselves!

It also depends on how high you hold up your clenched hands. If you hold them on your lap, it means that you are somewhat anxious or restrained. However, if you hold your clenched hands near your face, this means that you are more likely frustrated.

Praying hands.

If you hold your hands together like you are praying, but only the tips of your hands are pressed against each other, this is one of the most recognized signal of personal superiority and confidence.

You are the type of person that can make things happen because you think logically and you tend to look at things calmly... at least you think you are.

Of course, depending on other signals that you are sending out, this can also be interpreted as being clever, devious, or manipulative.

Rubbing the chin or neck.

If people are rubbing their chin and looking straight at you, all this means is that they are thinking. You've got them thinking, evaluating, and judging.

This is a good sign if you are trying to sell something because it indicates that at the very least you've got your message across.

If somebody is rubbing the back of their neck or tapping their fingers and looks like they are playing the piano on the table, this means that they are either bored, frustrated, or exasperated. These are not usually positive signs.

Whatever message you are sending out is not registering properly. Depending on how a person rubs his or her neck, it may mean that they are afraid, frustrated, angry, feeling threatened, or even intimidated by your presence or by what you are saying.

What you do with your fingers plays a big role in how other people will perceive what your message. Make sure that what you do with your fingers are consistent with the other signals you are sending out with the other parts of your body. People are holistic readers of body language. They pick-up on different clusters so you have to be very careful about the signals you are sending out.

6. Chest protection.

As you might imagine, the chest by itself is a bit harder than most other areas to read.

You can gesture wildly with your hands, and you can stand and wiggle on your legs. But you can't really move your torso or chest independently... so what can you gain from looking at someone's chest?

It's not about the actual movement of the chest – it's about how people hold and protect it.

Your chest is actually the most important part of your head behind your head. If someone was to make a movement or threat towards you, you would protect your face, hold your arms out, and turn your back to protect your chest.

Of course, this is for good reason. Your torso contains your heart and all of your vital organs, and is incredibly instinctual to protect.

Your heart can only withstand so much impact, and too much can easily lead to death. Next to your brain, your heart is the most important organ as far as life and death are concerned. Therefore, it is the most fragile aspect of your body, and it has been ingrained in us to protect it at all costs – even if you were to lose an arm!

So the body language of the chest and torso is not about the chest and torso itself, it's about how much people display or cover the chest. If you use your arms as armor for your chest, it is telling.

Unsurprisingly, most body language signals imply subconscious feelings about defensiveness, security, and protection.

It may seem harmless enough, but a simple crossing of arms or closing of the chest may indicate a supreme discomfort and feeling of danger in people! It's important to catch these feelings in people before they grow.

Crossed arms.

Crossed arms can mean a variety of things, but let's recall what we know about the chest. The chest is instinctually protected and covered when people don't feel 100% safe or comfortable.

You're protecting the core of your body from any perceived damage, and it's an automatic response.

The important part here is that perceived damage isn't just from obvious, outright dangerous situations like being yelled at or being afraid of someone.

This can extend to situations from actual danger, to simply just being impatient and yelling at people at hurry up.

If you are confronting someone and expecting them to retort back at you.

If you are talking to a professor and expecting

bad news.

If you are debating something with someone.

If you are giving someone a stink eye because they sat in the seat that you wanted.

You get it.

You don't even have to be talking to someone for the body language signals of the chest to show up to protect you.

Of course, it's entirely possible that some people are just fidgety and have trained themselves to cross their arms when they are bored or want to show that they are engaged in someone. You yourself might cross your arms because it's just the most comfortable position for you while you stand.

But as a general rule, how covered the chest and torso are indicative of the degree of comfort and security someone feels.

The more open and less covered a chest is, the more someone might also be wanting to display that there is comfort and that they are non-threatening in a situation. For example, clasping the hands behind the back.

And if the chest is open, uncovered, or even puffed out, it indicates a readiness and strength for whatever is coming their way.

However, there are slight variations to this rule.

<u>One crossed arm.</u>

When someone crosses one arm – leaves one arm hanging and the other across their chest grasping their elbow – it has been shown to indicate a lack of self-confidence and unfamiliarity. It's another degree or discomfort, and the end message is that the person is simply nervous in the environment.

You will see this often in people with a new group of friends, where they are uncertain of what to say, but also want to appear as open and friendly as possible.

They are probably trying to just fit in, but can't seem to find the words to say. This is an easy scenario to imagine, as it's one we are all familiar with. That person standing on the outside of the circle smiling and apprehensively trying to figure out how to blend in? We've all been there at some point in our lives.

One crossed arm can also indicate concentration and focus on a speaker or task at hand. It occupies the hands and arms and leaves all of the mental bandwidth for what's going on in front of them.

It's a way of shushing the rest of their body so their full attention can stay on something else – the equivalent of locking yourself into a room to work undisturbed.

Crossed arms with grasping hands.

Take the normal crossed arms position and add hands that are grasping the biceps of the other arm.

It's an extreme form of the crossed arms signal, and even though it may appear as though someone is trying to hug themselves, rest assured this is not an affectionate signal.

It typically means that this person needs reassurance badly. They feel a dangerous amount of insecurity, and are clenching their hands on their arms because that's the only form of security they can get. Literally and figuratively, their comfort lives in their fingertips.

It's like when you go on a rollercoaster, and you end up with sore fingers afterwards because you were clenching the handles around you so hard. Though you might have logically known that there was no real danger, your body subconsciously wanted to protect you and did so in a muscular way.

We might as well call this the rollercoaster arm cross.

An insider key to the rollercoaster arm cross is to examine how hard they are actually squeezing their arms. You can do this by looking at how white their fingers are. The whiter they are, the more blood has been displaced by the pressure of the squeezing, and the more insecure they feel.

Confident crossed arms.

While most variations of crossing arms tends to be about instinctively protecting the chest and vital organs, there are a few versions that project confidence and a feeling of authority over others.

A key variation concerns what the thumbs are doing while the arms are crossed. If the thumbs are sticking out while the rest of the fingers are buried, this has been shown to indicate a feeling of confidence and even dominance. This person feels that they can control the situation, and can signal to others that they feel a sense of authority, even if they don't actually possess it officially.

If you pair the thumbs with other confident body language signals, it can even indicate arrogance or cockiness, but as with many things in this book... it's going to depend heavily on context.

Let's not forgot the final interpretation of protecting the chest that actually has nothing to do with protecting the chest! Sometimes crossed arms are just a symptom of boredom, and trying to figure out how to leave a situation gracefully.

Remember that crossed arms by themselves shouldn't allow you to jump to conclusions. It is generally not a positive sign, but context is key, and body language signals must be read holistically.

<u>Leaning horizontally – bored.</u>

If someone's torso is more horizontal than vertical, IE leaning over, it can signal boredom and fatigue. For example, when they lean forward and rest their hands on their knees, lean on tables, or slump over counters. They simply don't have the energy to keep themselves upright and are subconsciously disengaging.

7. The poker face myth.

In what should be a surprise to no one, the face contains the most expressive body language signals on the body. Unless someone has made a concerted effort to study, learn, and overcome all subconscious movements, how someone's face looks and how people touch it will often be a key to their inner thoughts and feelings.

There's a reason that the **poker face** is so prized and difficult to truly learn, even for the most professional and lucrative of poker professionals. It's why so many of them still wear sunglasses when they play poker. It's just damn difficult to not have a facial tic or expression that shows what someone is really thinking.

The funny part about facial signals is that many people think that they know what the signals mean because they are so common and widespread – they're constantly written about!

Of course, this presents a huge problem. Just as with every other body language signal, such as crossing the arms, there is a ton of ambiguity, lack of clarity, and context-dependence in interpreting someone's facial signals... especially with close friends.

We can easily imagine this: you have a great friend and you've spent enough time with them to know that scratching their left eyebrow is indicative of fatigue and tiredness. This doesn't translate to others however, so we are left with blank slates for the most part for each individual.

Sometimes people are correct regardless, but the goal of this book is to present best practices and awareness of the most common interpretations of body language.

Facial signals are often tiny, but detectable with awareness and a little bit of practice.

Unconscious microexpressions.

Microexpressions are tiny facial expressions that we barely realize that we're making. They usually come from emotions that we want to hide, but aren't able to... and people don't typically feel the need to hide positive emotions.

So imagine that a friend has told you that she just went on a date with someone that you despise. The most positive remark you can squeeze out is "Oh... cool!" You think you didn't showed your displeasure.

But you'd be wrong. You'd likely **flash a slight frown for a tiny fraction of a second**. The thing with microexpressions is that true poker faces are nearly impossible.

If you're anticipating something pleasant to happen, you'll have a slight smile for a fraction of a second. The most common ranges of microexpressions are surprise, disgust, anger, happiness, confidence, and comfort, among many others. These microexpressions are often developed over time.

Of course, people do sometimes notice microexpressions, but their nature makes them extremely difficult to understand and interpret. Moreover, a lot of microexpressions are really combinations of many different facial signals.

You may be sending separate signals with your eyebrows, eyes, and smile, all combined into a series of microexpressions. So how can be break microexpressions into smaller components?

Eyebrows.

Eyebrows are very expressive and an easy signal to read. Raised eyebrows are typically signs of heightened awareness. If you are talking to someone and their eyebrows raise throughout the conversation, you have piqued their curiosity and said something to make them pay attention – for better or worse.

Key emotions to focus on when you see both eyebrows raise are interest, anger, joy, curiosity, and engagement.

Aside from heightened awareness, raised eyebrows is seen as a sign of friendliness and submission. It creates an effect of *'soft eyes*,' and is to show that you mean someone no harm, and come in peace. It's the kind of body language signal you might unconsciously do when you're meeting someone new, or approaching a puppy.

This is definitely not a negative aspect of submission – it just telegraphs that you want to be liked by others and that you are not a threat of any kind. This is the kind of body language signal that you want to send out to lubricate social situations, like closing a business deal, or flirting up a storm.

A single raised eyebrow has a much different meaning than when both eyebrows rise at the same time. A single raised eyebrow is also a much quicker, and momentary action, whereas both eyebrows being raised is something that is typically held. This indicates some degree or skepticism, shock, surprise, or novelty. As a general rule, the emotion to focus on is surprise at the reveal of something unexpected, for positive or negative.

Finally, when you lower your eyebrows, this is almost universally interpreted as menacing or threatening. In other words, you're angry or upset. In some cases, it can be interpreted as you feeling sad or feeling threatened.

Eye direction.

We've all heard that strong eye contact – a good balance between strong eye contact and breaking it, is ideal for creating trust and empathy.

But we also all know that most people don't do this, and unconsciously move their eyes in directions that can indicate a range of the emotions that they are feeling.

You're not going to be able to read them completely, but the following guidelines have been shown to be tested and true.

If someone is moving their eyes upwards to the right, this usually means that they're trying to recall something from their memory. They are trying to recollect something that they have seen in the past, and redirect their eyes to try to scan their memory. This is typically harmless, unless it is paired with some body language signals that might indicate that there is a lie brewing.

However, if someone is talking and their eyes drift to the upper left, this will usually mean one of two things. First, they might be imagining something creative, and be thinking about how to express themselves artistically. You can think of this mode as daydreaming.

Second, the eyes might drift to the upper left if they are actively lying to you. But of course, this is very contextual and best judged with paired with other signals.

You also have to take into account that studies have shown that very visual people tend to utilize the upwards left look while they are lying – because they are literally painting a fake memory for themselves to recite.

On the other hand, people who tend to be more auditory, or who tend to navigate the world and their feelings in terms of sounds, tend to talk while moving their eyes at the center level.

If they move their eyes to the right, they're essentially trying to remember something that they've heard in the past. If they tend to move their eyes to the left while they're talking, they're trying to imagine something that they've heard. Again, this may lead to supporting a conclusion that the person is lying. It all depends upon the question you ask them while they're talking.

People who tend to look at the lower corner of their eyes while talking are people who tend to navigate their emotions and the world, in general, through their feelings, taste, or smell. If they look to their lower right while they're talking, it means that they're trying to remember something that they've felt, tasted, or smelled in the past. If they are talking and they're looking to their lower left, they might be talking to themselves. They're going into an internal dialogue.

Finally, a non-directional tip. If someone appears to be squinting at you, it gives the indication of annoyance or skepticism.

<u>Glasses.</u>

One of the most common quirks people have when it comes to their face, and their eyes, is what they do with their glasses. A lot of people reposition their glasses on their nose while they're talking. You might think this is innocent and harmless. But in reality, it actually is giving away a lot of their thinking processes.

The good news is that when somebody is repositioning their glasses to the tip of their nose while you're talking to them, it means that they want to hear more.

This is actually a good sign because when somebody wants to hear more, they have a positive evaluation of what's going on. This is a crucial piece of information to know and understand if you're job, in any way, shape, or form, involves sales.

One of the most frustrating things about sales is that you don't necessarily know what's going on in the mind of your prospect. But when they reposition their eyeglasses on their nose, that's your cue to change your pitch a bit so you can give them the message they want to hear and make that sale.

Whenever you're talking to people, you have to remember that they're paying attention to more than the words that you're saying. In many cases, your message is really only interpreted based on the totality of the experience of talking with you. This involves your tone of voice, how excited you seem to be, your facial expressions, and your microexpressions. If you want to be a more effective communicator, you really have to be more aware of your microexpressions, and control them in such a way that they lead to a consistent interpretation.

8. Vocal delivery says more than the words themselves.

Effective communication from a body language standpoint is all about consistency. Other people, even your best friends, will never know all the facts that influence your moods and emotions.

Unfortunately, in this world, people have to make snap decisions.

This is why it is really important to make sure that you have clear control or at least a high enough level of awareness regarding these clusters of body language messages and signals you are sending out.

Far more than your actual words, your vocal tone of voice and vocal inflections are key to understanding and reading people's true intentions. The words and actual text of your communications are the first level of understanding – the way they are delivered is the second and deeper level.

It's what makes sarcasm, most types of humor, and inspiration possible. Modulating your delivery can convey literally anything you want, despite the actual words coming out of your mouth. It's just an approach that has somewhat more subtlety, and thus, many people don't always catch the real message that is being conveyed through vocal delivery.

Vocal delivery can engender trust. It can persuade and motivate. It can sell the lousiest product, just because of a vocal delivery that promotes trust and comfort.

Of course, your tone of voice is not going to be the ultimate deal-killer. In many cases, people make their decisions based on the totality of all the signals you are sending out. Still, it would be a big mistake on your part to completely overlook and ignore the power of the tone of voice.

Speed of speech.

This is first of all a matter of figuring out what a person's normal rate of speech is. If they just happen to be a hyper person that has a motormouth, you should take note of it. Likewise, if they happen to be from the South or talk like they have a mouth full of molasses (in the best way possible, of course), then you should take note of it, because determining someone's emotional state from their speed of speech is based on how they deviate from their normal speed!

When someone speaks slower than normal, it shows a certain amount of seriousness. They are taking the time and effort to carefully communicate an important piece of information. Of course, there comes a point of slowness when someone can appear as mentally slow, so there is sometimes a thin line.

To use this effectively, you must use it sparingly. If you recite everything slow and expect people to pay attention, that simply won't happen. It's like highlighting specific words on a page of text – if you highlight everything, it just loses the effect.

Use a slow and soft vocal tone when you are trying to emphasize a point. Don't overuse it.

Conversely, when someone is speaking quickly, it usually means that they are excited about something. You see this all the time in people who are speaking in public and in front of crowds. Their body is literally telling them to fear it, and that they should react by fighting or running – their adrenaline spikes, and sometimes this makes their voice and hands shaky with the excess of energy.

Excitement as a general umbrella covers nervousness, anxiety, the "jitters," and all such feelings. So it doesn't necessarily have to be a positive association. Just remember that a fast speaking tone is a byproduct of physiological changes in the body that speed the heartrate up, and make everything function faster and more efficiently out of some base excitement.

<u>High pitched tone.</u>

When you have a high pitched tone, it also indicates the excitement umbrella. Again, this doesn't necessarily mean excitement in a positive manner.

A high pitched tone is usually very easy to decipher because it will mostly be paired with other body language signals. There will typically be a very clear stimulus and source for the high pitched tone.

However, the negative part about the high pitched tone is how people might perceive you. A high pitched tone can be viewed as weakness, which consequently will make you look easy to excite, scare, or intimidate. You may be perceived as weak, emotional, and ultimately unstable.

Instability does not tend to make people trust or rely on you, so make sure to keep your excitability levels in check – through your vocal tone!

If you are trying to improve your overall communications performance, pay attention to your vocal tone. Make sure that there is a lot of variety in the vocal tones that you use. Most importantly, make sure that you use the proper vocal tone in the right context. You need to sound angry at certain times. You need to speak slowly and softly at other times. Make sure that you know the proper context of these vocal tones so you can use them for maximum gain and effectiveness.

9. Reading a man's body flirting.

As I've touched on before, context is always key when you are trying to read someone's body language... otherwise you run the risk of completely misreading that person.

An all-important context is love, flirting, and decoding if someone likes you. These are high stakes, and if you want to attract that man and present the opportunity of romance, you need to learn to read his body language carefully and accurately.

Unfortunately, the nature of flirting and attracting the opposite sex is that there are no clear green lights. People are far more indirect than they say they are, and flirting inherently is about hinting your interest without putting yourself out there for rejection and hoping that you can make them feel the same!

That's worth a repeat: there are no clear green lights with flirting body language.

You need to temper your expectations, look at the totality of circumstances, and make sure that you aren't reading something into neutral body language where there isn't anything – in other words, thinking someone is interested in you when they definitely are not.

Fortunately males tend to be a little more direct than females in their body language. They are also expected to pursue and take action more in the romantic sphere.

It's not hard to imagine that men and women have different body language signals in general, and in flirting no less. The different proportions of our bodies and the gestures we are socialized with make a huge difference in reading the opposite sex. For example, would a man kick one of his legs up while kissing his wife?

Gender differences highlighted.

As a general rule of thumb, males and females differ in but one respect: what actions make them appear sexy and attractive.

This might not always be noticeable at social gatherings, but just peek into a setting where people are vulnerable and exposed like at a beach. You'll see all of the following in full force.

Masculinity is all about power, dominance, and strength. Accordingly, men will subtly straighten their backs to appear taller and stronger, suck in their guts, and expand their chests. They will highlight their stature and muscles, while downplaying their neutral qualities. This is when men become very 'alpha' in body language and gesticulation.

Femininity on the other hand is all about sensuality, allure, and curves. When women want to appear flirty or are around those that they find attractive, they will accentuate their sexual characteristics such as their cleavage, long hair, and hips. This will cause them to push their elbows together, cross and uncross their legs to emphasize their length and the curve of their hips, flip their hair, and walk with exaggerated swaying of the hips.

Something that both genders will do before and during an encounter with someone that they are interested in, however, is groom themselves in small ways. Males will fix their shirt collars, ties, and make sure that their flies are zipped. Females will fiddle with their jewelry, adjust their hair, and decide if her legs look better crossed or not.

Fidgeting.

Hopefully this is something that's already on your radar.

Fidgeting in men, like women twirling their hair or swinging their leg, is often a sign of being nervous. Contextually with the opposite sex, fidgeting and nerves are a sign that a man wants to impress someone, and isn't 100% confident in how he comes off to her… which is most guys.

It's the same case as before with excitement and anxiety – the body's physiology gives them a jolt of extra energy and adrenaline at the prospect of talking to someone that they like, so the extra energy and adrenaline comes out as a fidget.

Common fidgets for men in the presence of women that they are interested in are: touching their face a lot, readjusting positions, shifting their weight and alternating between leaning on something, playing with their hands, playing with anything that they are holding, running their fingers through their hair, and checking how their clothes are fitting right in front of you.

Eye signals.

Men are often more direct than women when it comes to attraction. They are also much more visually stimulated than women.

Put those two things together, and you'll find that men's gazes are often very telling about how they feel about you. Historically, men were hunters so they had to rely a lot on their eyesight and graphical information.

But just because they are graphically attracted

doesn't necessarily mean that they are romantically attracted.

However, you can be damn sure that he is attracted to you, at the very least – and that of course is the first step to liking you.

I'm going to put on my dating coach hat for a second here and say that if a male is attracted to you – if he would sleep with you if given the chance – there is a good chance that he'd be willing to date initially too.

If you can catch him peeking at you in a very shy way, that they seem to be stealing glances, that might indicate romantic attraction. This is also the kind of glance that people throw at circus freaks, however, so it could just indicate that he's curious about something.

Duration and the manner in how a man looks at you has everything to do with the nature of their attraction.

And of course, if there is a lack of eye contact, it's not likely he is simply playing hard to get... he's probably just not that into you.

Arm placement.

If a man has his arms crossed at you, it doesn't necessarily mean that he's feeling defensive about you. Remember, body language is highly contextual, and if he's in the romantic and flirting context, crossed arms can mean a few things.

Crossed arms on a man can indicate that he wants to disengage with you, and he is literally putting something between you and him to try to stop the conversation. If you pair this with a lean backwards, then this is likely the case.

However, paired with leaning towards you, he could just be looking to shrink the size of his silhouette to appear less threatening.

This is something that we see in the animal kingdom constantly. Animals will stretch out their limbs or wings to appear larger when they want to make an impression or dominance and intimidation – think peacocks and bears rising on their hind legs. Correspondingly, animals will also shrink themselves when they want to appear friendly and nonthreateningly – think dogs lowering their head so low that their chins are on the ground when they approach smaller dogs and human children.

A final interpretation of crossed arms is that the male is taking a position of control and strength by framing his body with his arms. Framing the body with the arms is strong because it puts his arm muscles out front as a mating display.

Let's run with this for a second. You can interpret this as a man who is trying to take control of the conversation. This is a guy who is confident, knows what he wants, and likes being in control. He probably won't be passive, and will present a challenge to you in the best way possible.

A guy who crosses his arms confidently won't just roll over for you, and this is great if you are looking for a guy who can stand his ground.

That's a lot to read into a simple crossing of the arms, but let's not pretend that everyone doesn't do the same!

Tone of voice.

Remember the vocal delivery rules from the previous chapter? Guys who speak quickly are excited. In the romantic context, this means that they are excited and nervous about something in front of them. It could be you.

Volume is also an indicator of interest. The louder, the more excited they are to talk to you sometimes.

Laughter: if he's doing it, even to jokes or simple statements that weren't that funny, it's a huge sign of interest. They just want to create positive feelings and associations with you, and that's exactly what laughing at your jokes does. It makes you feel good about yourself, and we all enjoy people that seem to like us as well. It's a smart psychological play.

The lean.

A final simple body language signal for men and their romantic interests is to observe how much he is leaning towards you. This can be when he is standing or sitting, but the more he is leaning towards you, the more engaged he is with you and wants to continue the conversation.

The way to see this is not always in his upper body – you need to look at how he is shifting his weight, and whether it is on his front foot towards you. While sitting, this is shown by putting his elbows on his knees towards you, or if there is a table, putting both of his elbows on the table towards you.

You can also test how engaged he is trying to be by playing yo-yo with your bodies. That is, you can lean back or take a step back and see if that causes him to lean more towards you immediately. Then take another step back and see if he follows you, in a sense.

Men and women differ quite dramatically in terms of body language in the context of romantic attraction. While we both subscribe to the same general vocabulary of body language signals, the context, the setting, and other smaller body language signals all combine to produce differences in meaning. Read carefully, as you don't want to overstep... or miss out on a guy who was sending very subtle signs of interest!

10. Reading a woman's body flirting.

Guys, I know.

Women are confusing to read for many reasons.

Part of the reason is the way that genders are socialized differently, it is acceptable for women to be more passive about their romantic intentions. They rarely make the first move, and this impacts their body language signals highly.

This means that many women are used to telegraphing interest in subtle ways because society has deemed it unladylike for them to be aggressive and direct. This allows them to steer clear of the possibility of rejection and appearing aggressive at all.

If you as a male have ever felt strung along by a female, it's possible that the simplest explanation was that their signs were so subtle that you literally could not interpret them... if they were even there.

This knowledge alone should clear up some things for men. Very rarely will you get a clear green light from women, so you'll have to read into their actions more than you might want to.

Of course, this is not without negative consequences. If you interpret a body language signal of interest incorrectly, then you risk a supremely awkward moment of rejection... but that's the price we pay as men to play!

Because men are typically the pursuers, women have also developed many mechanisms to let men down gently and diplomatically.

Thus, even if a woman knows even if the world ends and the guy she has just rejected would come in second place to the last remaining chimp, she will still convey that diplomatically and apologetically. However, you could probably interpret her negative feelings by seeing how she stands, her posture, and various other body language signals.

Two totally different messages, but the truth is often revealed by our body language. What body language signals will be helpful in determining if a woman is romantically interested in you?

Eye contact.

Eye contact is one of the few ways that women can directly indicate interest, and thus some are actually quite bold about it.

So if a woman is making strong eye contact at you, take that as a clear sign of interest. If she is keeping eye contact with you, and keeps her gazes lingering before she turns to another direction, take that as a clear sign of interest. All of these paired with a big smile are positive signs.

It's not just the duration of eye contact that

will signal a woman's interest – it's the fact that they will have a smile in their eyes and a certain entertained look. Simply holding eye contact with someone is slightly offputting and robotic, after all.

If the pupils are dilated, it indicates relaxation and comfort around you. On a certain level, it means they also trust you!

If there is a lack of emotion or smile in the eyes, it can indicate that you have her attention... but not anything further, such as romantic or flirting interest.

A final note on eye contact from women.

Nerves, anxiety, and shyness will be present many times when they are around men that they like, so they may avert their eye contact as a result of that anxiety. They won't feel comfortable holding eye contact with you, and might feel a heightened level of self-consciousness.

Arm placement.

Crossed arms in the romantic context can be

very different for women than they are for men.

If a woman is crossing her arms and her hands are grasping the outer part of her shoulders or arms (like she is cold), then it is a defensive position and she is uncomfortable and anxious.

However, if she has her arms folded with her thumbs inserted in her arms with her other fingers sticking out, this means that she feels comfortable and confident in the conversation. She sees herself as a participant and an equal partner in the conversation and this is a good sign. This indicates that this person trusts that you are not creepy, intimidating or uncomfortable to be around. This can lead to further openness in terms of romance.

What about normal crossing of arms? For women, it's more of a neutral position that doesn't indicate much. Although many people equate having an open body position to a woman being more interested in you, crossed arms are too open to interpretation for me to posit anything.

On one hand, crossing of the arms can frame and create cleavage, which is obviously a sign of interest. On the other hand, it can be like a recoil away from someone.

Finally, what about arm placement on you?

In other words, if a woman is touching you... well you should know that this is positive. As I mentioned before, women don't usually make aggressive gestures or motions towards guys that like – they are subtle. So if a woman is touching you, even in subtle ways like brushing your arm or hitting you playfully, take that as a strong hint of interest. For them, a subtle touch might be equivalent to putting our arm around them as a male.

You just need to make sure that she isn't amazingly flirty and touchy with everyone she knows.

Leg placement.

If a woman is sitting down and is shaking her foot, this can either be a sign of boredom, or a sign of anxiety and interest.

You have to look at what other signals the shaking is paired with. If her foot is pointed at you and is shaking very slowly, it means she is interested in you. If she is also looking at you with a smile in her eyes, and her tone of voice is somewhat slow, or she is giggling somewhat nervously.

However, if she is just shaking her leg very quickly, this might just mean that she is bored or she is just looking for excitement and this might not necessarily mean she is interested in you romantically.

Fingers.

Pay attention to a woman's finger. If she placed them on a table and is tapping like she is playing a piano, this means that she is either looking for you to step-up the excitement of the conversation or come up with something new. She could be bored and not interested in you.

However, it would also be helpful to refer to the prior chapter about fidgeting and occupying their hands.

Tone of voice.

More specifically, her laughter.

If she is giggling an inordinate amount, or laughing at jokes that you know aren't that funny, it's usually a good sign of interest. I mentioned this before, but people unconsciously strive to make others like being around them. Laughing with tem is a sign of validation and makes people friendlier to us because you seem more agreeable. Women are no exception to this.

Reading a woman's romantic body language signals takes a lot of practice. You should take this and the previous chapter together as one because there are just many signs that people will use, and everyone will feel inclined to use different signals.

It's not a matter of women using masculine signals or vice versa – people just act in ways that they've learned throughout their lives that will convey the message that they want, and it's not always conscious or gender-aligned!

11. Lie detection 101.

What's the last white lie you told?

Maybe it was when you got your morning coffee, and you said that your terrible day was going well when the barista asked how your day was going. Inconsequential stuff.

So what's the last big lie you told?

People lie every day. Maybe it's because they don't like telling the truth, they like to stretch the truth to fit their purposes, or because they love embellishing stories to make them seem more dramatic or interesting.

Whichever the case, people aren't always as honest as you might hope. And when it comes to money, relationships, and romance, lying isn't something you should make a habit of.

Unfortunately, people are never going to step up and confess that they're lying or that they tend to take liberties with the truth. In many cases, if you catch them in a lie, they will try to wiggle their way out of it through either more lies or verbal gymnastics. The good news is that you don't have to expect people to admit that they are lying for you to know.

You only need to pay attention to certain telltale body language signals of deceit that they are sending out.

Deceitful body language.

The beautiful part about detecting lies is that most of us are incredibly unprepared to lie.

Human communication is largely unconscious, and the words coming out of our mouths comprise only a fraction of the message that is actually received. We've all learned how to make our body language consistent to some degree, but given how few of us actually understand how to do that effectively... even fewer actually understand how to lie without their body language giving them away.

People can control the words they use to lie, but typically not the subtle signals that their bodies will communicate, or even the way they say the words.

People are not born liars. We are not preprogrammed to lie. In almost all cases, lying is a learned behavior. It is not in our human nature to instinctively lie. Since we are not wired to lie, our body language is often out of step with the parts of our being that we have trained to lie.

So what are these signals of deceit and lying? Everything and anything from your vocal tone to your eye placement, your eye movement, your facial expression, your body positioning, your posture, and all points in between.

Hand over mouth.

There are two things we can draw from our childhood experiences here.

First, we were always told that lying was something to avoid. It was a bad habit that you would be punished for.

Second, if a curse word slipped out of your mouth as a child, a common habit was to put your hand over your mouth as if to literally stop the flow and cram it back inside.

These two things amount to the covering of the mouth as an involuntary reaction when someone instinctively knows they've committed a wrong. Putting your hand over your mouth is like reliving your childhood, and that habit is still inside our minds somewhere.

So when you hear someone say something questionable, followed by them involuntarily touching their mouth or covering it to some degree, there's a fair chance that they just told a lie.

They knew they were going to do it, but they couldn't help it, and on some degree wish they could take it back. Put another way, it's like they've shouted an obscenity in the middle of church, depending on how big the lie is. They feel the unconscious need to do right and take it back, and their body language betrays what the mind has decided to say and do.

They might even speak their lie through a hand over their mouth. Any movement of the hands near the mouth is telltale.

Shushing finger.

Another common body language signal of deceit is for people to put a finger over their mouth as if they are telling people to "shh" in a movie theater. It can involve one or two fingers.

This is similar to the hand over the mouth – the hand over the mouth signals that they feel like they should not have said that internally. The shushing finger signals that they feel like they should be quiet on the lie that they have just told, and either said it more softly or not at all.

Fidgets around the mouth are extremely telling, as it's the body's way of expressing an inconsistency right at the root of the source where words actually come out.

A common variation of this is when people

fake cough after a lie. It's a cough born out of nervousness and anxiety, and is used to draw attention away from the lie.

I mentioned earlier that people are not naturally wired to tell lies. When we say something incongruent with how we actually feel, this causes massive confusion for the body, and many body language signals of deceit are the result of this confusion an anxiety.

Scratching your nose.

When people lie, there are certain physiological changes that take place. One of them is that there are changes in blood flow due to the adrenaline and anxiety that comes with the discomfort of lying.

This sudden change in blood flow can cause discomfort and irritation in many areas, and the nose is the primary area in which this surfaces.

So when someone is rubbing their nose a lot, minus allergy season, there is a good chance that they either feel some anxiety about what they are saying, or they are flat out lying.

Covering eyes.

Lying is very uncomfortable for most people. When people lie, they just want to get it over with and hope that no one challenges them on it. The best way of trying to slip something by people is to draw as little attention to it as possible – covering the eyes and avoiding eye contact is a great way to do this. See no evil.

So when someone is talking, try to keep track of where their eyes are going. Are they going side to side, are they physical covering their eyes with their hands, or are they avoiding eye contact? This doesn't necessarily mean that the person is lying, but something is making them uncomfortable.

They might also keep rubbing their eyes to distract from the words they are speaking.

It might not mean lying, but it's still a form of evasion, especially when combined with an unwillingness to make eye contact.

The theory that liars avoid eye contact is actually a tip that many people are familiar with, so liars may focus on not avoiding eye contact when they lie.

However, they will usually skew too far the other way and hold unnatural strong and constant eye contact, as it to convince others of their trustworthiness.

You must be on the lookout for too much eye contact *and* too little.

Too much blinking can also be a giveaway of lying – anxiety and nerves can express themselves in the eyelids as well!

Pulling an earlobe.

Just like with the nose, blood flows easily and quickly to the ears when the body knows that there is something to be concealed, like a lie. Just think about how quickly your ears get hot when you get self-conscious or feel embarrassed about something.

If someone is pulling their earlobe, playing

with it, or even just brushing it, it could be an indication of deception. At the least, it indicates that something has changed physiologically within the person, and that change usually comes from some kind of anxiety or confusion.

Neckplay.

The neck is probably the most vulnerable spot on a human. A single slice and someone can bleed to death within a minute. We all know this instinctively, so our instinct is always to protect our neck.

When we want to feel protected, we protect our neck and turn our back. It's comforting and makes us feel better about ourselves.

You can see why this might matter in lying – lying makes us uncomfortable because we feel nervous about it.

However, when they are doing the talking and you see them constantly scratching their neck, either they have a skin condition or they are doubtful or uncertain regarding the stuff that is coming out of their mouth.

The shakes.

For many people, lying isn't simply uncomfortable. It's amazingly stressful, and the body has intense reactions to emotional stress.

Just think about the last time that you were going to make a big speech. Your palms were probably sweaty, you had butterflies in your stomach... but the biggest physical manifestation was that you had the shakes. Your hands were shaking, your knees might feel like you were on a boat, and your voice was unsteady and weak.

The bigger the speech, the more you were likely to get the shakes... and so it is with lying. The bigger the lie, the more emotional stress is being induced, and the more the body produces excess adrenaline to deal with it, which results in shaking of the voice and hands.

The key with detecting lies is that the emotional state that lying puts people is in a state of stress. Stress finds a way to the surface physically, and those are some of the body language signals that I've outlined for you.

Too many details or tangents.

A final sign that you're dealing with a liar is that they quickly jump off of the topic that they are lying about.

For example, if they are telling a lie about going skiing, they will focus on a small detail of the skiing trip, or jump to a new topic entirely. This is to keep the period that the lie is in the air as short as possible.

This is because they know that their story or statement is false, and the longer they stay on it – this can only lead to three things.

First, it can lead inconsistencies in the story if it is examined further, which will expose the person as a liar.

Second, staying on the lie longer will increase their anxiety levels, and even if the story isn't exposed, more physical body language signals of lying will surface.

Finally, the other person will be forced to weave a web of lies to support the initial lie, and this is something that creates even more internal conflict and anxiety.

12. Body talk around the world.

Just like body language has entirely different meanings dependent on the context, culture is also a huge determinant of what body language ends up conveying.

You might think you are sending out a certain signal, but if you find yourself in a different cultural environment, you might actually be sending out the opposite message. If you want to maximize the effect of the body language signals that you are sending out, you have to gain awareness of cultural differences.

Some cultures are very indirect and express themselves through avenues other than their words – these cultures place a ton of value on body language and use it as a secondary means of talking.

Other cultures are more direct, and what someone says is what they mean! These cultures might focus less on body language, if there is usually a clear verbal message.

Still, no culture is completely immune from utilizing body language signals in order to make sense of the idea that you are trying to communicate.

Eye contact.

The presence and meaning of eye contact differs quite a bit between eastern and western cultures.

As we've explored in this book, direct eye contact with someone in a western culture is taken as a sign of strength, trust, and comfort. It shows that you are sincere, that you are straightforward, and that you are open.

At the very least, when you look people in the eye, it proves that you're not being evasive. The lack of eye contact will lead you to mistrust their intentions.

In many eastern cultures, this is essentially flipped. Utilizing direct eye contact in an eastern culture can be seen as disrespectful, as averting the eyes is a sign of respect in many business and familial contexts.

Although western influence and business practices continue to spread to the east to the point where eye contact is sometimes expected, timing and duration is still important. Held eye contact can even be viewed as a threat or challenge by the holder... and if you fixate on the eyes, it may even spiral towards disrespect and threatening.

Accepting things.

It should be prefaced here that eastern cultures are far more about formality in respect, and their body language signals reflect that.

In the West, when somebody presents you their business card, you take the card; you thank the person for giving you their card, and you quickly put in your pocket with one hand or put it in your wallet.

That's pretty straightforward and very businesslike.

In the East, however, there is a special ritual that you need to go through. If you deviate from this ritual, you may be viewed as a rude, thoughtless or offensive person. Not exactly the kind of signals you want to send out, especially if you're trying to get business done.

First, you take the card with both hands. You can't just take it with one hand like you would in the West. After you take the card with both hands and while you are holding the card, you say, thank you. In certain cultures, primarily in Northeast Asia, you might need to bow while you say thanks.

You keep holding on to the card while talking to the person. This is a sign of respect and importance. You can't quickly put the card in your wallet or your pocket. If you do that, it shows that you didn't really put much importance in the card. That's a quick way to lose a business deal.

This phenomenon of accepting something with two hands is also reflected in receiving gifts, money, and when someone is pouring you a beverage in eastern cultures, so be aware of all contexts! It shows respect, and acknowledgment that someone is doing you a favor, whether they are or not.

Pointing.

This again highlights the difference in levels of respect between eastern and western cultures. If you're making a presentation in the west, it's completely acceptable to point at someone. It's even acceptable to point at someone while you're talking to someone to make a point or emphasize something.

However, in the east, pointing is an aggressive sign. It's very much saying "HEY YOU, YES YOU" and however far the finger extends out is how threatening it is. Thus, it's more than disrespectful, it's challenging.

A related sign to the point, the OK sign, also carries significant differences in meanings in other cultures. Using it in the west, it simply means an acknowledgment or acceptance of a statement.

But used in South America, the OK sign is actually a very nasty insult that basically tells the person to kiss your ass. Brazil in particular adheres to this meaning.

Cultural differences play a big role in body language. Make sure that you are aware of the cultural context and setting where you make these body language gestures in. Culture and context go a long way in how you will be received. Be very careful regarding the overall signals that you are sending out.

Conclusion

There may not be a single takeaway point from this book other than that the body talks in mysterious ways.

There are uncountable interpretations based on people's assumptions and life experiences... but remember Professor Mehrabian's experiment from the introduction of this book?

So many body language signals are innate and natural that there are **some** objective standards, and many of the techniques in this book are offshoots of those.

The more you combine your own life experiences with the knowledge in this book, the more you will be able to precisely pinpoint what someone is feeling, perhaps even before they realize it themselves.

Truly grasping body talk is a lifelong process, but I believe that what is presented in this book can serve as a foundation for a better, master communicator version of yourself.

Detecting lies, decoding the opposite sex, and reading anyone like a book?

Put in the work, combine your observations with the content of this book, and they will simply be inevitable side effects of learning body talk.

Sincerely,

Patrick King
Social Skills and Conversation Coach
www.PatrickKingConsulting.com

P.S. If you enjoyed this book, please don't be shy and drop me a line, leave a review, or both! I love reading feedback, and reviews are the lifeblood of Kindle books, so they are always welcome and greatly appreciated.

Other books by Patrick King include:

CHATTER: Small Talk, Charisma, and How to Talk to Anyone
http://www.amazon.com/dp/B00J5HH2Y6

26783923R00068

Printed in Great Britain
by Amazon